THE STARTING POINT LIBRARY

SCIENCE

Wet and Dry

THE DANBURY PRESS

A Division of Grolier Enterprises, Inc.

©1973 Macdonald and Company (Publishers) Ltd.
First American Edition 1977
Library of Congress Catalog Card Number: 75-7431
Printed in U.S.A.

123456789987

On wet days the rain falls.
The clouds are very grey.
The girl splashes in a puddle.

2

On dry days the sun often shines.
The sky may be clear.
Sometimes there are small white clouds.

3

Can you see any of these clouds today?
Are they high or low?
How are they moving?

4

rain-gauge

top turned upside-down

cut

plastic bottle

You can measure how much rain falls.
You can make a good rain-gauge
from a plastic bottle.

On wet days we need waterproof clothes.
How many waterproof things can you
see in the picture?

6

Collect all kinds of fabric.
How long does it take a spoonful of
water to drip through each kind?

Roofs keep the rain out.
Look at different kinds.
What materials are used for making roofs?

Sometimes we use materials which
soak up water.

Cut strips of different fabrics.
Which soaks up water the best?
Try it with different kinds of paper too.
10

Weigh a brick. Leave it in water for an hour. Weigh it again.

Does a brick soak up water?
How much?

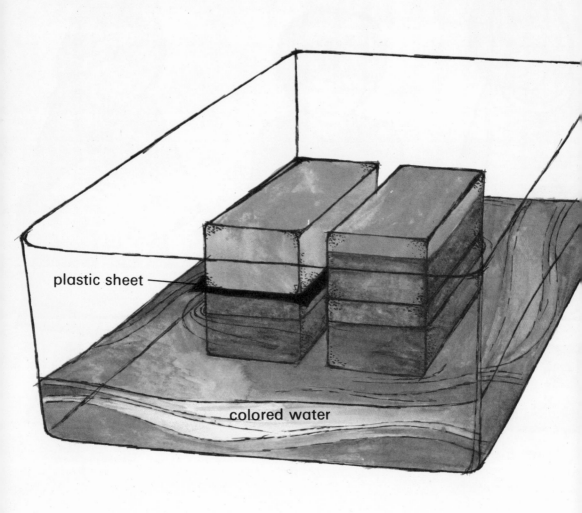

plastic sheet

colored water

Why is one top brick wet
and the other dry?
12

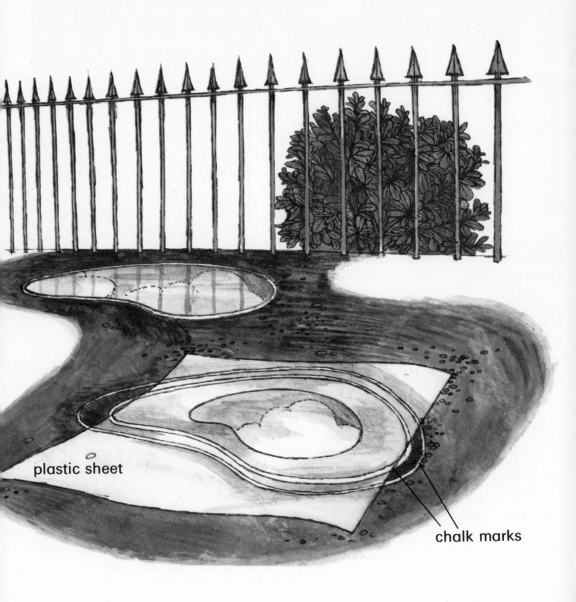

plastic sheet

chalk marks

After rain, chalk around a puddle.
Draw around it again after an hour.
Do the same with a puddle on plastic.
Where does the water go?

13

Put jars of water in different places.
See that the jars are all the same.
Mark the water level.
Look at the water level every day.

Put the same amount of water
in different shapes of jars and dishes.
Which water evaporates first?

Seas, lakes, rivers and puddles evaporate.
You cannot see the water vapor.
Up in the air it cools to tiny drops.
Then you see clouds.

Someone forgot to water this plant.
Plants need water.
The roots take it in from the damp soil.

Weigh some soil.
Let it dry for several days.
Weigh it again.
Was there a change in weight?

18

Try soils from different places.
Weigh out the same amount of each.
Dry for the same time in the same place.
Weigh again.

These plants grow in damp places.

These plants grow in drier places.

You can find these animals in damp places

These animals like dry places.

Stir these things into jars of water.
Watch what happens.

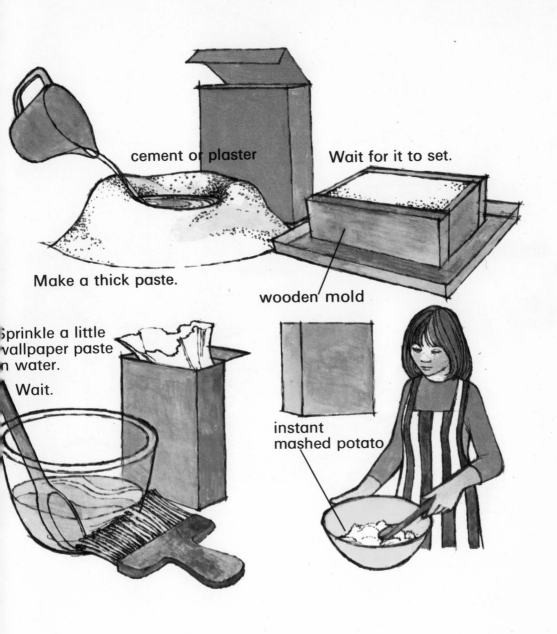

cement or plaster

Wait for it to set.

Make a thick paste.

wooden mold

Sprinkle a little
wallpaper paste
in water.

Wait.

instant
mashed potato

Some things change when mixed
with water.

What does water do
to iron and steel things?
What has water done
to this wooden fence?
What can we do to stop this?

cracks in lawn

Roll out some wet clay, to fit on a ruler

wet hair

dry hair

Dissolve plenty of salt in water.
Leave it in a **warm place**.

How does drying change things?
What happens to the clay on the ruler?
Let the salt water dry up slowly.
What do you see?

Index

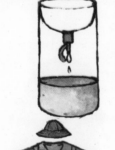
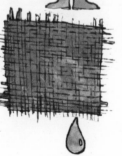